FINDING A VOICE:
Women's Fight for Equality in U.S. Society

THE WOMEN'S LIBERATION MOVEMENT, 1960–1990

TERRY CATASÚS JENNINGS

FINDING A VOICE:
Women's Fight for Equality in U.S. Society

THE WOMEN'S LIBERATION MOVEMENT, 1960–1990

TERRY CATASÚS JENNINGS

MASON CREST
PHILADELPHIA

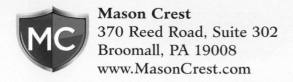

Mason Crest
370 Reed Road, Suite 302
Broomall, PA 19008
www.MasonCrest.com

Printed and bound in the United States of America.

CPSIA Compliance Information: Batch #FF2012-8. For further information, contact Mason Crest at 1-866-MCP-Book.

First printing
1 3 5 7 9 8 6 4 2

Library of Congress Cataloging-in-Publication Data

Jennings, Terry Catasús.
  The women's liberation movement, 1960-1990 / Terry Catasús Jennings.
    p. cm. — (Finding a voice: women's fight for equality in U.S. society)
  Includes bibliographical references and index.
  ISBN 978-1-4222-2358-1 (hc)
  ISBN 978-1-4222-2368-0 (pb)
  1. Feminism—United States—Juvenile literature. 2. Women's rights—United States—Juvenile literature. I. Title.
  HQ1410.J45 2012
  305.42—dc23

                              2011043488

Publisher's note: All quotations in this book are taken from original sources, and contain the spelling and grammatical inconsistencies of the original texts.

Picture credits: courtesy Boston Women's Health Book Collective: 43; Franklin D. Roosevelt Presidential Library: 28; Getty Images: 14; © Jeff Nagy/iStockphoto.com: 16; Library of Congress: 3, 8, 11, 13, 22, 25, 26, 31, 37, 39, 41, 47; Lyndon B. Johnson Presidential Library: 32; photo courtesy of Marine Corps Base Camp Pendleton Combat Camera: 41; courtesy National Organization for Women: 35; RetroClipArt: 18; Ronald Reagan Presidential Library: 50; Aspen Photo / Shutterstock.com: 48; Helga Esteb / Shutterstock.com: 51; Benjamin F. Haith / Shutterstock.com: 45; StockLite / Shutterstock.com: 52.

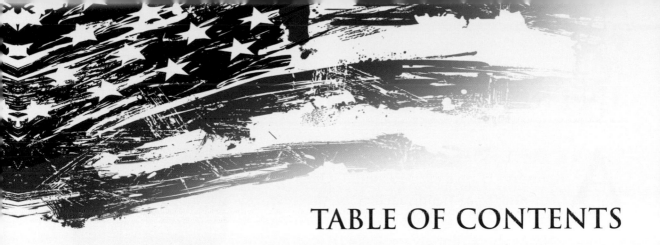

TABLE OF CONTENTS

INTRODUCTION

A. Page Harrington, director, Sewall-Belmont House & Museum

As the Executive Director of the Sewall-Belmont House & Museum, which is the fifth and final headquarters of the historic National Woman's Party (NWP), I am surrounded each day by artifacts that give voice to the stories of Alice Paul, Lucy Burns, Doris Stevens, Alva Belmont, and the whole community of women who waged an intense campaign for the right to vote during the second decade of the 20th century. The original photographs, documents, protest banners, and magnificent floor-length capes worn by these courageous activists during marches and demonstrations help us bring their work to life for the many groups who tour the museum each week.

The perseverance of the suffragists bore fruit in 1920, with the ratification of the 19th Amendment. It was a huge milestone, though certainly not the end of the journey toward full equality for American women.

Throughout much (if not most) of American history, social conventions and the law constrained female participation in the political, economic, and intellectual life of the nation. Women's voices were routinely stifled, their contributions downplayed or dismissed, their potential ignored. Underpinning this state of affairs was a widely held assumption of male superiority in most spheres of human endeavor.

Always, however, there were women who gave the lie to gender-based stereotypes. Some helped set the national agenda. For example, in the years preceding the Revolutionary War, Mercy Otis Warren made a compelling case for American independence through her writings. Abigail Adams, every bit the intellectual equal of her husband, counseled John Adams to "remember the ladies and be more generous and favorable to them than your ancestors" when creating laws for the new country. Sojourner Truth helped lead the movement to abolish slavery in the 19th century. A hundred years later, Rosa Parks galvanized the civil rights movement, which finally secured for African Americans the promise of equality under the law.

The lives of these women are familiar today. So, too, are the stories of groundbreakers such as astronaut Sally Ride; Supreme Court justice Sandra Day O'Connor; and Nancy Pelosi, Speaker of the House of Representatives.

But famous figures are only part of the story. The path toward gender equality was also paved—and American society shaped—by countless women whose individual lives and deeds have never been chronicled in depth. These include the women who toiled alongside their fathers and brothers and husbands on the western frontier; the women who kept U.S. factories running during World War II; and the women who worked tirelessly to promote the goals of the modern feminist movement.

The FINDING A VOICE series tells the stories of famous and anonymous women alike. Together these volumes provide a wide-ranging overview of American women's long quest to achieve full equality with men—a quest that continues today.

The Sewall-Belmont House & Museum is located at 144 Constitution Avenue in Washington, D.C. You can find out more on the Web at www.sewallbelmont.org

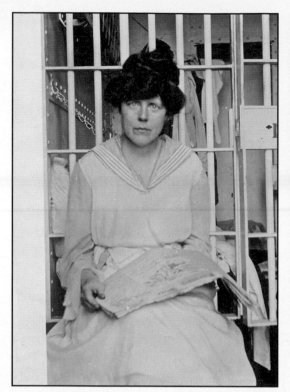

By the early 1960s, the struggles of early 20th century woman's rights leaders like Lucy Burns (top left) and Alice Paul (top right) had been largely forgotten by many Americans.

1

HOW COULD THEY FORGET?

On November 15, 1917, Lucy Burns was jailed. Beaten, she spent the night standing, chained to the bars of her cell, her arms above her head. When she and her friend Alice Paul went on a hunger strike—they refused to eat—their jailers forced food through tubes in their noses. The two women struggled, enduring pain and humiliation, until the jailers finally gave up.

Burns and Paul weren't the only women who suffered—many others were jailed and tortured as well. Their crime? They wanted suffrage, the right to vote. Lucy Burns and Alice Paul, along with earlier suffragists like Susan B. Anthony, Elizabeth Cady Stanton, Lucretia Mott, and Carrie Chapman Catt, dedicated their lives to the fight for women's equality.

Thanks to their efforts, women did gain the right to vote in 1920, when the Nineteenth Amendment was ratified. Over the next four decades, though, the sacrifices of Burns, Paul, and other suffragists were all but forgotten. Betty Friedan, who wrote an influential book called *The Feminine Mystique*, noted that "the first century of struggle for women's rights had been blotted out of the national memory."

With the publication of Friedan's book in 1963, the women's movement in America was rekindled and a second period of activism began. From

1960 to 1990, women worked to gain equality with men under the law. They achieved greater opportunities in the job market and in education. They demanded, and received, control over their own bodies. Thanks to these gains, many women found greater self worth.

During the 1960s, thanks to the women's movement, new laws gave American women many new opportunities. In the 1970s, by taking advantage of the laws, the movement began to nudge attitudes towards equality. By the 1980s, women were beginning to see the fruits of their labors.

WHY DID WOMEN NEED THE VOTE?

Until the mid-1800s, when the suffrage movement began, American women had few rights. For instance, before 1848 in many states a married woman could not own property. Anything she earned, inherited, or brought to the marriage became her husband's property. Those who held power—men—believed that women were inferior both physically and mentally. Women could not be trusted to make important decisions, so they could not vote or serve on juries. Those who were tried for crimes were judged by men, never women. The only profession a woman could pursue was teaching; and that was only if she was unmarried. With laws favoring men, and with few opportunities to earn money, it was next to impossible for a woman to get out of a bad marriage.

Suffragists wanted the vote so they could elect representatives who would try to change the laws that kept women enslaved.

FAST FACT

The U.S. Constitution, ratified in 1787, did not prohibit women from voting. However, by 1807 all 17 states in the union had passed laws denying women the right to vote.

During the early 20th century, women marched and demonstrated hoping to generate support for a constitutional amendment that would give the right to vote. This photo was taken in 1915.

THE ROAD TO SUFFRAGE

The suffrage movement began in 1848. Elizabeth Cady Stanton and Lucretia Mott were abolitionists—people who wanted to see the end of slavery in the United States. They recognized that the rights and freedoms they sought for African-American slaves were rights that were denied to women also. That year, Stanton and Mott organized a convention in Seneca Falls, New York. Those who attended agreed on a "Declaration of Sentiments." This document argued that "all men and women are created equal," and insisted that women should have the same rights as men, including the right to vote.

From that beginning, suffragists protested and lobbied for the vote. Their work intensified after the end of the Civil War in 1865. The Fourteenth Amendment (1868) and Fifteenth Amendment (1870) gave African-American men the rights of U.S. citizens, including the right to vote. The women who had worked for passage of these amendments were disappointed that rights for women were not included in these laws. In 1872 Susan B. Anthony was arrested and jailed for casting a vote for Ulysses S. Grant during the presidential election. Before her trial, she said, "It is a downright mockery to talk to women of their enjoyment of the blessings of liberty while they are denied the use of the only means of securing them provided by this democratic-republican government—the ballot." Despite this, Anthony was found guilty and fined.

It took many years, but the work of suffragists eventually led to passage of the Nineteenth Amendment to the U.S. Constitution. This amendment, ratified in August 1920, gave women the right to vote.

WE HAVE THE VOTE, NOW WHAT?

Suffrage was not the same as equal rights. Laws would need to be passed to give women the same rights men enjoyed. Some women tried to secure those rights with another amendment to the constitution. Beginning in 1923, the Equal Rights Amendment was introduced at every session of Congress. However, opponents of the amendment generally prevented Congress from voting on the legislation.

When women gained the vote, they didn't tend to vote for issues as a unified group. They also had no strategy for electing women to Congress. There were not many women candidates for high political offices in any case. Many women did not even consider themselves worthy of the job. The number of women who had experience in law, government service, or running a large business—traditional credentials for a politician—was very small. But without women in Congress to advocate for women's rights, women could never hope to gain full equality with men.

Even so, from the 1920s through the end of World War II, American women gained more freedoms. Flappers, the liberated young women of the

A woman rivets the fuselage of a bomber in a California factory, 1942. During the Second World War, millions of women entered the workforce.

1920s, smoked and drove cars, drank illegally, and dated without chaperones. Growing numbers of women went to college or worked outside the home. Two million more women went to work in the 1930s during the Great Depression. After the United States entered World War II in December 1941, women went to work in even greater numbers. They replaced men in factories, banks, the government, and wherever they were needed. Women also served in responsible positions in the armed forces.

A funny thing happened, however, after the war ended in 1945. Rather than continued gains in the percentage of women finishing college and pursuing careers, there was, in fact, a decrease over the next 20 years. Society pushed women away from careers and towards marriage, home, and children. Why this reversal?

During the 1950s and 1960s, middle-class women were expected to happily raise their children and take care of the home, while their husbands were the primary breadwinners.

2

A WOMAN'S PLACE IS IN THE HOME

According to Betty Friedan, during the period from 1945 to 1960 it seemed as though American women were under a spell. Friedan called this spell the "mystique of feminine fulfillment"—the things that American society believed women should do in order to be happy.

BACK TO "NORMAL"

When the soldiers came home from the war, women were pushed aside so that men could have their jobs back. Some women moved into lower-paying, less important positions. Others happily returned to the traditional lifestyle of women, being mothers and housekeepers. After the turmoil and fear of the war, Americans were ready to return to their normal lives.

During the late 1940s and early 1950s, in American society "normal" could be defined as couples reuniting after long years apart, or young men and women getting married and having children. Thanks to a period of economic prosperity, for many middle-class women "normal" also meant a house in the suburbs filled with newfangled, labor-saving appliances. To be "normal," women were expected to stay home and take care of the house and children while their husbands worked. Women heard this message everywhere.

In addition, women were also told that it was not "normal" to want a professional career outside the home. Psychologists and other experts in

In American history, the period from 1946 to 1964 is known as the "baby boom," because of the unprecedented number of children—over 77 million—born during this time. "The suburban housewife—she was the dream image of the young American woman," wrote Betty Friedan about the prevailing social attitude of the period. "Their only dream was to be perfect wives and mothers; their highest ambition to have five children and a beautiful house."

human behavior issued reports blaming working mothers for a variety of social problems, from juvenile delinquency to cowardice in battle. These messages about women and the workplace stuck, even though they were false and unfair. They were part of the "feminine mystique."

WORKING FOR "PIN MONEY"

The prevailing attitude in American society was that women had no ambition to have a career or a profession. At the time a common stereotype of women was that they were less intelligent than men. They were also considered to be less able to cope with stress. Most people wanted to believe that a middle-class woman only worked for "pin money"—a little extra money that she could use to buy small items for herself—or so she would not be bored at home once her children started school.

Employers were wrong about working women, though. Most women who worked did so because they had to. Some women were the only bread-winners in their families. Others worked to help raise their families into the middle class, or to provide their children with a college education. Sometimes women worked to support husbands who were attending college or graduate school.

PROTECTIVE LEGISLATION

During the late 19th and early 20th centuries, it became more common for women to work. In the garment and textile industries, women made up most of the workforce. These were factory jobs. They paid low salaries and required long, hard hours. They often took place in unsafe conditions. Children as young as six years old worked in factories, too.

Over the years, reform groups fought to pass labor laws to help women and children. By the 1920s, child labor was restricted and many workplace safety laws were in place. State laws limited the number of hours that a woman or child could work at certain jobs. Other laws restricted the amount of weight women could lift. Some laws mandated rest periods, or prohibited women from working at night. Others guaranteed a minimum wage.

The laws were meant to help women and children, so they became known as "protective legislation." However, an unintended side effect of pro-tective legislation was that men and women were treated differently in the workplace. This reinforced negative stereotypes about women, such as that they were less intelligent or capable then men. Protective legislation also reduced the number of higher-paying jobs open to women. It was not until the 1960s that federal legislation granted women a measure of equality in the workplace, as well as the legal standing to enforce such laws in court.

Women were generally discouraged from working at "white-collar" sales or office jobs, or in professions like law, medicine, or engineering. Many people believed, falsely, that men could do these important jobs better than women. Those women who became professionals were often steered to less-challenging career paths. Women physicians were expected to be pediatricians, rather than surgeons. Women journalists could write features for the society pages, not cover "serious" news or write editorials.

In addition, women were told that if they worked, they would take jobs away from men who had families to support. Newspapers and magazines urged women to leave the jobs for returning soldiers. Employers often paid women less than men for doing the same job. They justified this by saying that the male employees were responsible for providing for their families. Employers often did not provide health or retirement benefits to women workers, assuming that their husbands would provide these benefits.

BUY, BUY, BUY!

After World War II, industries changed from making planes and tanks to making appliances. Since the country needed to keep industry going to maintain a strong economy, women were encouraged to fill their homes with the newfangled gadgets. Advertisements told them these gadgets would make them happy. Also, during the Cold War, the government pushed the idea of a strong family to fight the spread of communism. By contrasting the happy, capitalist, American family  in its appliance-filled suburban home with the drab, oppressed communist family, our government aimed to prove that our capitalist system was better.

Most damaging, employers rarely considered hiring women for important jobs or promoting them to executive positions. These employers, mostly male, did not believe women were intelligent or emotionally stable enough to be trusted with important decisions. Employers also feared a woman would quit her job when she became pregnant.

These employment practices were unfair and harmful. They prevented women from earning a living wage and from reaching their full potential. As a result, many women who might have gone to work stayed home instead. Young women who went to college often dropped out to get married. Many never used their education in a professional capacity.

Even colleges and universities discouraged women from pursuing careers. In the 1960s, women admitted to medical schools made up less than 10 percent of each entering class. Law schools admitted just one woman for every 20 students. At the beginning of every school year, the president of Radcliffe College told the incoming students that their college education would "prepare them to be splendid wives and mothers." As late as 1964, a U.S. Labor Department publication stated that it was not "the policy of the Women's Bureau to encourage married women and mothers of young children to seek employment outside the home."

NO WAY TO ESCAPE THE MESSAGE

The attitude that a woman's place was in the home, and that all women could be fulfilled through motherhood and housekeeping, permeated all aspects of American society during the 1950s. Religious leaders preached that women should be stay-at-home wives and mothers. Popular magazines told young women how to catch and keep a man, since this was the only source of their happiness. Wives were expected to accept their husbands' authority without question.

Women were not viewed as individuals, but as an extensions of their husbands. It was common for married women to introduce themselves using their husbands' names—for example, Mrs. John Smith or Mrs. Ken Short, rather than Jane Smith or Betty Short. Whether they worked or not, women accepted their role. Even if women had a good job, they didn't dare make too much of it; their husband would not be seen as a good provider.

Women who weren't married were pitied. According to a *Saturday Evening Post* poll, "96 percent of married women opted for marriage—and 77 percent of single women agreed." Professional women were looked at with suspicion. Many had remained single or childless to pursue their career. What kind of person would give up the happiness of raising a family in exchange for a job?

ALL A MYTH

Although marriage, children, and a house in the suburbs were supposed to be the keys to happiness, they weren't for many women. These women identified with Betty Friedan when she wrote, "We can no longer ignore that voice within women that says: 'I want something more than my husband and my children and my home.'"

Each woman thought that there was something wrong with her because she didn't want to be just a mother and housewife. Her physician told her she was mentally unbalanced if she wasn't happy. Women didn't realize that they had been fed what Friedan called the feminine mystique—and that it was difficult to be happy living a myth.

3

EXPOSING THE MYTH

I t was inevitable that American women would realize that their happiness did not exist *only* in the home and in having children, or that their treatment in the workplace was unjust. For a number of reasons, the decade of the 1960s was a fertile time for women to change their place in American society.

By the early 1960s, the baby-boom mothers had teenagers at home. As *Harper's* magazine said in an issue about women, "whether one finds it richly rewarding or frustrating, there is one trouble with motherhood as a way of life. It does not last very long." Now that their children were getting older, these women had time to ponder. Many didn't like the way their lives had turned out. While husbands found meaning in work and professions, middle-class women without children to raise found little meaning in life.

The discontent may not have been obvious, but it was real. When *McCall's* magazine ran an article in 1956 entitled "The Mother Who Ran Away," the response was huge. A few years later, in 1962, *Redbook* magazine ran a contest titled "Why Young Mothers Feel Trapped." The magazine received 24,000 entries, many of which expressed deep, strong feelings. American women were not just unhappy, they were depressed. They consulted psychiatrists in unprecedented numbers.

THE FEMININE MYSTIQUE

In 1963, *The Feminine Mystique* put a name to the dissatisfaction that many women felt. In the book, Betty Friedan wrote:

> I came to realize that something is very wrong with the way American women are trying to live their lives today. I sensed it first as a question mark in my own life . . . There was a strange discrepancy between the reality of our lives as women and the image to which we were trying to conform, the image that I came to call the feminine mystique.

The mother of three children, Friedan had continued working part-time as a freelance writer while her children were growing. She wrote for labor publications as well as for women's magazines. The idea for *The Feminine Mystique* came from a 1957 survey she had taken of women who had graduated with her from Smith College 15 years earlier. Because Smith was a prestigious college for women, Friedan expected to find that many of her former classmates were professionals who were happy about their careers.

Instead, she found that most of her classmates had stayed at home, and they weren't happy. They, like Friedan, felt caught between the American ideal of a happy housewife and mother and the reality of an unfulfilled life.

Her idea for an article on these women was turned down by several magazines. The (male) editors couldn't believe that what Friedan had found was true. Instead

Betty Friedan (1921–2006) was a leading figure in the feminist movement of the 1960s and 1970s. Her 1963 book *The Feminine Mystique* started a conversation about women's place in U.S. society.

of giving up, Friedan expanded her research to include female graduates of other colleges, as well as women in many walks of life. Instead of continuing to pitch the idea as a magazine article, she wrote the book.

In *The Feminine Mystique*, Friedan explained that there was no evidence to support the theory that the children of working women often became delinquents or were emotionally troubled. She described the sadness women felt at having given up their dreams of careers in order to have a family, and told them that they still had options. Women who read the book learned they were not alone in what they were feeling. The frustration and restlessness that had been simmering inside them, now bubbled out. Her book is credited for providing the spark that ignited the women's movement in the early 1960s.

A TIME OF GREAT CHANGE

The early 1960s was a time of both hope and turmoil in the United States. Many people were optimistic about John F. Kennedy, a young and charismatic politician elected president in 1960. They expected his administration to work toward a fairer, better American society. At the same time, African Americans were protesting for civil rights. They wanted the same

NOT LIKE MOM

During the 1960s, young people began to rebel against the values and beliefs that their parents represented. Many were opposed to what they considered the materialism of the 1950s. While stay-at-home-moms were struggling with their personal dissatisfaction, younger women were looking at their own mothers' lives and wanted no part of them. According to Anna Quindlen, a novelist and columnist who came of age during the late 1960s, "By the time I was a grown-up, the answer, if you were strong and smart and wanted to be somebody, was not to be a mom."

rights as white Americans. The atmosphere of protest and the emphasis on human rights provided the perfect launching pad for what was called the second wave of the feminist movement—women's liberation.

During the 1960s, college campuses were alive—first with civil rights protests, and later with protests against the Vietnam War. Many white students joined the fight against race discrimination. Women activists in both the civil rights and the antiwar movements mobilized friends and acquaintances to join the protests. They worked to get the attention of newspapers and local television stations.

Unfortunately, many of the young women who became involved in these movements for change found that an old problem remained: men didn't take them seriously. Two white activists who were involved with a civil rights organization called the Student Nonviolent Coordinating Committee (SNCC), Mary King and Casey Hayden, wrote about this problem. They compared the subordinate, second-class position of blacks in American society to the position of women:

> The average white person finds it difficult to understand why the Negro resents being called "boy," or being thought of as "musical" and "athletic," because the average white person doesn't realize that he assumes he is superior. And naturally he doesn't understand the problem of paternalism. . . . Assumptions of male superiority are as widespread and deep-rooted and every much as crippling to the woman as the assumptions of white supremacy are to the Negro. Consider why it is in SNCC that women who are competent, qualified, and experienced are automatically assigned to the "female" kinds of jobs such as: typing, desk work, telephone work, filing, library work, cooking, and the assistant kind of administrative work but rarely the "executive" kind.

Some women achieved responsible leadership roles by becoming involved in romantic relationships with movement leaders. However, the responsibility and leadership opportunities usually vanished when the relationship ended. Rayna Rapp, an activist with the group Students for a Democratic Society (SDS), later commented that men "had all this empathy for the Vietnamese, and for black Americans, but they didn't have much empathy for the women in their lives."

Both white and African-American young women can be seen participating in this 1965 civil rights march from Selma to Montgomery, Alabama.

Being involved in the civil rights movement taught young women like King, Hayden, and Rapp a great deal. As they became more aware of injustice and discrimination faced, women became more interested in changing American values and ideas to create a society in which men and women were equal partners.

CHANGING ATTITUDES TOWARD SEX

In the American society of the 1950s and early 1960s, young women were expected to abstain from sexual relations prior to marriage. One reason for this was that premarital sex could result in unwanted pregnancies. An unwed mother would have a difficult time supporting a family. There was also a social stigma. An unmarried girl who became pregnant would feel shame and disgrace.

During the 1960s, however, an important change occurred: the birth control pill first became available in the United States. Although some methods of birth control had previously been available, none were as reliable as "the pill," nor as easy to use. It was liberating. With the pill, women had more opportunities to pursue a career because they could plan pregnancies, limit the number of children they had, and decide when to have them. Being able to experience intimate relationships outside of marriage without fear of pregnancy brought women almost the same freedom in relationships enjoyed by men.

Author Helen Gurley Brown expressed that feeling of liberation in her 1962 book *Sex and the Single Girl*. The book's main idea was that "a single woman could support herself [and] have fun, independence, and a full sex life."

MARGARET SANGER AND THE PILL

Margaret Sanger (1879–1966) was a nurse. Working in New York City, she dedicated her life to birth control education because she believed that controlling reproduction meant freedom for women. She was the founder of Planned Parenthood, an organization to teach families how to limit the number of children they would have. She established birth control clinics. Sanger was arrested and served time in jail for spreading birth control information, but her efforts opened the door for doctors to provide information about birth control. She was the driving force behind funding the research for a birth control pill. In 1960 that pill became a reality. By making it easier for women to prevent unwanted pregnancies, the pill opened the way for greater participation by women in the workplace.

4

WORKING FOR CHANGE THROUGH LEGISLATION

I n 1960 there were 3.5 million more women of voting age than men. Such numbers meant women could have had a significant impact on a presidential election. Unfortunately, most women tended to vote in the same way as their husbands. In an article in the *Saturday Evening Post*, Sidney Shalett asked, "Is there a Women's Vote?" She urged women to "insist on speaking and acting as individuals who have a rightful place in the human planet."

But while for most women voting and working for their rights was still a few years in the future, during the early 1960s a few courageous congresswomen and some women in high positions in the government began working quietly for equality through the law.

COMMISSION ON THE STATUS OF WOMEN

One of these government workers was Esther Peterson. In 1961, President Kennedy placed her in charge of the Women's Bureau of the U.S. Department of Labor. A labor organizer and advocate, Peterson had worked for unions that represented teachers and garment workers. In her new position, she helped to convince the president to form a special commission that would look into workplace discrimination against women.

Key members of the Presidential Commission on the Status of Women included (left to right) Katherine Ellickson, Eleanor Roosevelt, and Esther Peterson. Roosevelt (1884–1962), who chaired the PCSW, was internationally recognized as an advocate for human rights. Peterson (1906–1997), the commission's vice chair, had a long and distinguished career as a supporter of women's rights in the workplace. Ellickson (1905–1996), a labor union economist and officer, served as executive secretary to the PCSW.

In 1961, President Kennedy issued an order creating the Presidential Commission on the Status of Women (PCSW). Members of this group, both male and female, came from Congress and the Kennedy administration. The PCSW also included respected scholars, representatives of trade unions and professional organizations, leaders of religious groups, and others. Former first lady Eleanor Roosevelt, who had served as a U.S. delegate to the United Nations and had helped write a document called the "Universal Declaration of Human Rights," was appointed the group's chairperson. Peterson was chosen as vice-chair.

An important member of the Presidential Commission on the Status of Women was Pauli Murray, an African-American lawyer and writer. Since the 1940s, Murray had worked against racial segregation. Murray saw that the women's problems were very similar to the problems experienced by

African Americans. She was convinced that to gain their rights, women would have to convince government representatives, just as civil rights activists had. Part of Murray's work as a commissioner involved cataloging the laws that prevented women from reaching true equality.

Catherine East worked for the Women's Bureau of the Labor Department, and Mary Eastwood and Sonia Pressman were lawyers for the federal government. They worked with the commission. Because of their government work, these women were prohibited from advocating for any political cause, including women's rights. However, with their knowledge of the system, they helped to facilitate the steps that were to come.

The commissioners had no power to act, but the group brought together high-achieving women in a way that had never been possible before. Sharing their experiences, these women began to understand the depth of discrimination against women. In a report issued in October 1963, the Presidential Commission on the Status of Women documented and criticized discrimination against American women in the workplace. The PCSW report, called *American Women,* pointed out the need for support services for working women, and called for changes in education, social security, childcare, and employment practices.

Before the report was issued, the American government had taken steps to address a widespread injustice: unequal pay for women. According to Labor Department statistics, in the early 1960s women workers earned

FAST FACT

In 1963 Esther Peterson pushed for the Equal Pay Act of 1963. Although the act mandated equal pay for equal work, it was still difficult for women to be considered for high-paying jobs. There was also no way of forcing employers to follow the law. More was still needed to push women towards equality in the workplace.

DEFINING SEX DISCRIMINATION

In 1965, Pauli Murray and Mary Eastwood co-published an important article in the *George Washington Law Review* titled "Jane Crow and the Law: Sex Discrimination and Title VII." The comprehensive article was about discrimination against women that was legally permitted.

The term "Jane Crow" was a reference to the so-called "Jim Crow laws," which were meant to keep blacks segregated from whites. Many states, particularly in the South, had passed these types of laws after African Americans obtained the right to vote in the 19th century. Among other things, Jim Crow laws prevented blacks from sharing restrooms, schools, and even seats on a bus with whites. The federal Civil Rights legislation of the mid-1960s was meant to eliminate the Jim Crow laws and racial discrimination. Murray and Eastwood believed that existing laws were perpetuating discrimination against women.

Murray and Eastwood wrote that men did not believe they were causing women any harm by placing them in subordinate roles, but that this prevailing attitude was wrong. "[When the law] gives men a preferred position by accepted social standards, and regulates the conduct of women in a restrictive manner . . . it relegates [women] to inferior status," they wrote.

In the article, Murray and Eastwood provided data showing that women were heads of 10 percent of all households in the United States, and they argued that more women were feeling the effects of sex discrimination in the 1960s than in previous decades. Women were disadvantaged because state and local laws prevented them from working at certain higher-paying jobs. They cited a number of examples, including laws that prevented women from working as bartenders or miners, at jobs that required heavy lifting, or at jobs that involved working late hours.

Women were considered second-class citizens in other ways as well, they noted. A woman had to asked to be considered to serve on a jury. Many state-supported colleges would not accept women students. Murray and Eastwood noted that equality for women did not require men and women to use the same public restrooms, and that it would not force women to leave their families and serve in the military. Instead, wrote Murray and Eastman, "we are gradually coming to recognize that the proper role of the law is not to protect women by restrictions and confinement, but to protect both sexes from discrimination."

about 59 cents for every dollar earned by men doing the same work. In June 1963, President Kennedy signed the Equal Pay Act of 1963 into law. The Equal Pay Act made it illegal for employers to give men and women different salaries for doing the same jobs. However, there was no way to enforce the act. The difference between men's and women's salaries would rise at a slow but steady pace during the 1960s.

TITLE VII

It was a political maneuver that was later called a joke, but Title VII of the 1964 Civil Rights Act was the stroke of luck that turned the tide of women's rights. When the act was poised to give African American men equal rights in the workplace, Howard W. Smith, a Virginia Congressman, added Title VII, a paragraph prohibiting sexual discrimination at work.

Smith hoped that by adding what he felt was a ridiculous right for women, he could stop a law that would benefit African Americans.

Smith didn't count on Martha Griffiths, a lawyer and member of Congress. She was interested in Social Security regulations that discriminated against women. When it came to the Civil Rights Act, Griffiths would not be stopped. "I made up my mind," she said, "that if such a bill were going to pass, it was going to carry a prohibition against

During the 1960s, Congresswoman Martha Wright Griffiths (1912–2003) of Michigan was the "leading advocate of women's rights in the House of Representatives."

President Lyndon B. Johnson speaks to the nation before signing the historic Civil Rights Act of 1964. The legislation created a new agency called the Equal Employment Opportunity Commission, which years later would work to ensure that women had equal opportunities in the workplace.

discrimination on the basis of sex, and that both black and white women were going to take a modest step forward together." Griffiths corralled enough votes to pass the bill through the House of Representatives. Senator Margaret Chase Smith took care of the Senate. On July 2, the Civil Rights Act of 1964 passed, including Title VII.

THE EQUAL EMPLOYMENT OPPORTUNITY COMMISSION

The Civil Rights Act created a new government agency called the Equal Employment Opportunity Commission (EEOC). The EEOC could use the Justice Department to prosecute employers accused of discrimination. However, although the EEOC was committed to resolve cases involving race, the agency tended to ignore cases of discrimination against women. According to EEOC lawyer Sonia Pressman, "we had an agency with a mandate to prohibit sex discrimination . . . in a country that was not conscious of the fact that women were the victims of discrimination."

For example, the EEOC refused to outlaw advertisements classified by gender: "Help Wanted—Men" or "Help Wanted—Women." These segregated ads prevented women from being able to apply for many higher-paying jobs in which they would now be paid equally. The EEOC's reason: segregated ads were easier for newspaper readers.

It wasn't until feminists pressed the issue that the EEOC began to change. Martha Griffiths spoke before Congress, exposing the EEOC's lack of action for women. "I would remind them that they took an oath to uphold the law, not just the part of it that they are interested in."

In the second half of the 1960s, many of the women who had been quietly working for women's rights through legislative changes decided they had to make themselves heard. The Third National Conference of Commissions on the Status of Women, held in 1966, seemed like a good place to start.

FAST FACT

Between 1960 and 1966, Congress considered 432 pieces of legislation on women's rights. Not all of them were passed, but it was a huge step forward.

5

I AM WOMAN, HEAR ME ROAR

The mood of the country was changing, and women were changing along with it. With the 1964 Civil Rights Act, the Civil Rights movement changed direction away from protest and toward making the new law work for African Americans. The Vietnam conflict was now a full-blown war and protests were hotter than ever. The women who had been quietly working for women's rights organized themselves and the young radical women who had been working in the Civil Rights and antiwar movements decided to do something about their inferior status.

NATIONAL ORGANIZATION FOR WOMEN

Through the fame Betty Friedan had received from her book, she was asked to address and participate in many government functions. Through those, she met and befriended women like Pauli Murray, Catherine East, Mary Eastwood, and Sonia Pressman. She called them the "underground network of women in Washington."

Although the original Presidential Commission on the Status of Women had ended its mission in 1963, the bond between the women who participated in it remained. At the third National Conference on the Commissions on the Status of Women in June 1966, a group of about 15 people met in Betty Friedan's hotel room. They wrote a resolution to require the EEOC to enforce Title VII. When the resolution was not allowed to be brought up for discussion before the whole conference, the group decided to form an organization for women. It needed to work for women's rights the same way that the National Association for the Advancement of Colored People (NAACP) worked for African Americans' rights. At lunch, Betty Friedan wrote "National Organization for Women" on a napkin. It wasn't only a name, but a call to action—now. The organization was born.

In 1967, NOW drew up a mission statement at its organizing conference: "To take action to bring women into full participation in the mainstream American society now, exercising all the privileges and responsibilities thereof in truly equal partnership with men." They elected Betty Friedan as president.

NOW's first priority was employment issues and enforcement of Title VII. The organization supported flight attendants (then called stewardesses) in their fight against discriminatory practices by airlines. In November 1966, the EEOC ruled that airlines could no longer fire stewardesses at age 35 or if they married. Women came to NOW for help in fighting for their rights in court. Volunteer lawyers worked round the clock to meet their needs. The NOW legal defense fund helped women who were denied higher paying jobs due to protectionist laws to successfully sue Colgate-Palmolive and Southern Bell Telephone Company. They pressured President Johnson to extend affirmative action programs to women. With this step, in 1967, government agencies and any businesses which worked

FAST FACT

The 1970 song "I Am Woman," co-written and performed by Helen Reddy, became an anthem for the women's liberation movement.

FAST FACT

When Southern Bell Telephone Company refused to hire a woman to a position that required heavy lifting, NOW's lawyer, only five feet tall and weighing around 100 pounds, carried the equipment in her hand while she delivered her statement to the jury.

for the government were required to choose a woman over a white man if their qualifications were equal.

The group also publicized women's issues by organizing marches and protest events. NOW picketed the *New York Times* and dumped newspapers in front of EEOC local offices to protest segregated ads. By 1968, want ads stopped referring to gender. They burned aprons at the locations in Washington, D.C. where suffragists had chained themselves to the White House Fence during their fight for the vote. They desegregated male-only bars and restaurants by staging sit-ins.

NOW, however, did not represent all women. In the beginning, they had no interest in lesbian rights. It was primarily an organization of older, professional women. A young woman activist, Meredith Tax, said:

> My friends and I thought of NOW as an organization for people our mother's age. We were movement girls, not career women; NOW [wasn't] radical enough for us. We wanted to build a just society...we didn't trust anyone over thirty.

RADICAL FEMINISM

Younger women wanted to challenge more than laws. They wanted to change the way America thought and challenge men's privileged positions in society. While the older women, the members of NOW, called themselves the women's movement, women's liberation was what the young radicals were all about.

In 1968, Jeannette Rankin, who had served two terms in Congress, led women to protest the Vietnam War in Washington, D.C. That same day, nearby, 500 women held the first National Women's Liberation Conference. The women who went to this conference were younger, and less likely to be professionals. Their ideas spread to cities and towns. Their goal was not to pass sweeping laws, but to create organizations to deal with specific issues at a local level. At consciousness-raising groups, women

GLORIA STEINEM AND *MS.*

Gloria Steinem was the granddaughter of a famous suffragist, Pauline Steinem. As a journalist, she exposed the terrible working conditions of *Playboy* bunnies by working as a bunny for three weeks. When she covered a meeting of the Redstockings, a women's liberation group, for *New York* magazine, she was hooked. Now she realized how much discrimination she had endured, from having lost assignments to male writers with less experience to putting up with "a lifetime of journalists' jokes about . . . wives, dumb blonds and farmers' daughters . . . in order to be one of the boys." She was proof that you could be both an attractive woman and a feminist. In 1972 she founded *Ms. Magazine*. The magazine reached women who might not otherwise have read feminist literature or become involved in radical feminist groups. According to Steinem, *Ms.* was a "how-to magazine for the liberated female human being—not how to make jelly, but how to seize control of your life."

would share ideas with each other and decide on strategies and actions. They pressured employers to provide day care for working mothers. They formed rape crisis hot lines and opened women's centers. They formed lesbian rights groups, as well as organizations dedicated to everything from legal aid to physical health for women.

In 1968 and 1969, radical feminist groups protested against the Miss America Pageant. They complained that such pageants have a negative effect on society because of their emphasis on beauty as a woman's most important characteristic. Feminists also protested against magazines like *Playboy*, which portray women in a demeaning way. Americans began to take notice of the radical feminists. In response to protest, the magazine *Ladies' Home Journal* began printing a section on women's liberation. When feminists took over a radio station, women's programs were added. The feminist project "Take Back the Night" shone the spotlight on rape in cities throughout the country.

EQUALITY FOR BLACK WOMEN

At the same time as white feminists, African-American women were working to gain their rights. Some women, like Pauli Murray, Eleanor Holmes Norton, and Shirley Chisholm worked by trying to change laws. Other women followed the radical path.

During the 1950s and 1960s, African-American women couldn't concentrate on women's liberation because civil rights for all African Americans took priority over women's rights. Black power made black men more powerful than they had been before. Men even expected women to be breeders to supply an army that would help in the struggle. Leaders of The Third World Women's Alliance (TWWA), an African-American radical women's group, stated "that in any society where men are not yet free, women are less free because we are further enslaved by our sex."

Many African American women were afraid to join the white movement. TTWA women told white activists that "until you can deal with your own racism and until you can deal with your OWN poor white sisters, you will never be a liberation movement."

In 1968, Shirley Chisholm (1924–2005) of New York became the first African-American woman elected to Congress. She served in the House of Representatives from 1969 until 1983.

Radical African-American feminists like Frances M. Beal worked on the issues that troubled their communities. They wanted to take control of their bodies and their reproductive rights. They wanted to help poor people, end racism, and stop police repression. While a student at the University of Wisconsin, Beal had joined The Student Nonviolent Coordinating Committee (SNCC) a civil-rights organization dedicated to eradicating Jim Crow laws. In the late 1960s she founded SNCC's Black Women's Liberation Committee (later renamed the Third World Women's Alliance). Beale's 1969 essay "Double Jeopardy: To Be Black and Female" expressed the view of African-American feminists that black women faced a harder road to equality than white women, because they suffered from discrimination on the basis of their race as well as their gender. Black women needed to become "teachers, doctors, nurses, electronic experts, chemists, biologists," wrote Beal. "Black women sitting at home reading bedtime stories to their children are just not going to make it."

6

POLITICAL AND LEGISLATIVE CHANGES

The 1970s were a time of great accomplishments for the women's liberation movement. There were also low points and disappointments along the way. Because of different perspectives, in some cases a triumph for some women meant a setback for others.

THE WOMEN'S STRIKE FOR EQUALITY

In 1970, Betty Friedan, along with other members of NOW, African-American feminists, and leaders from the women's liberation movement came up with an idea to draw attention to women's issues. At four o'clock on the afternoon of August 26, 1970, women were encouraged to leave their jobs or homes and take part in a march. The event—called the Women's Strike for Equality—was a triumph. Thousands of women marched in New York, Los Angeles, Washington, D.C., and many other cities, demanding equal opportunity in employment and education. A huge banner saying "Women of the World Unite" was sneaked into Ellis Island and draped on the Statue of Liberty.

Such demonstrations were impressive, but NOW founder Betty Friedan believed that women needed to take a larger role in politics if the women's liberation movement was to survive. In July 1971 she joined Gloria Steinem,

African-American activist Myrlie Evers, Congresswomen Shirley Chisholm and Bella Abzug, and others to announce the formation of the National Women's Political Caucus. The organization dedicated itself to increasing women's participation in all areas of political and public life—as elected officials, judges, lobbyists, and voters. The organization, which is still active today, soon established chapters in every state dedicated to moving issues important to women to the forefront of American politics.

Feminists recognized that not only did they need to elect representatives who were sympathetic to their cause, they also had to prevent those who opposed it from gaining powerful political offices. In one notable instance, in 1970 President Richard M. Nixon nominated Judge G.

BELLA ABZUG (1920–1998)

The first Jewish woman member of Congress, Bella Abzug was known for her brash personality and her trademark hats. In the early sixties, she founded the Women's Strike for Peace against testing of nuclear weapons. Later she worked on the Women's Environment Development Organization. Abzug not only co-founded the National Women's Political Caucus, she also pushed numerous women's bills through Congress. Among them were bills that gave women the right to manage their own finances, and better their Social Security benefits. She sponsored a bill for comprehensive child-care. In 1975 she led the fight which successfully modified the Civil Rights Act to include gay and lesbian rights.

The increase in women in politics made change easier. According to Abzug, "We put sex discrimination provisions into everything. There was no opposition. Who'd be against equal rights for women?"

Harrold Carswell to fill a vacancy on the U.S. Supreme Court. Feminists considered Carswell to be sexist. They noted that he had ruled in favor of the Martin Marietta Corporation, which had refused to hire a qualified woman simply because she had children. His ruling was later reversed by the Supreme Court in the landmark case *Phillips v. Martin Marietta Corp*, which called the practice sex discrimination.

Under the Constitution, the U.S. Senate is required to confirm, by majority vote, all presidential nominations to the Supreme Court. Feminist groups like NOW urged women to ask their senators to block Carswell's nomination. Betty Friedan spoke before the Senate Judiciary Committee. She said, "It would show enormous contempt for every woman of this country . . . if you confirm Judge Carswell's appointment."

The nomination was blocked, and Carswell's name was withdrawn. In his place, Nixon nominated another judge, Harry Blackmun, who was easily confirmed by the Senate. Blackmun was known as a conservative, but his views changed over time. In 1973, he would write the opinion in a landmark Supreme Court case of vital interest to the women's liberation movement: *Roe v. Wade*.

REPRODUCTIVE RIGHTS

In addition to seeking equal pay with men and greater access to jobs and education, women in the 1960s and 1970s wanted to secure what became known as "reproductive rights." These include the right to legal or safe abortion, the right to use birth control, the right to access quality healthcare, and the right to make decisions about pregnancy and childbirth without coercion, discrimination, or violence.

During the 1940s and 1950s, states began to do away with laws that outlawed certain forms of birth control. In 1965, the U.S. Supreme Court ruled in *Griswold v. Connecticut* that a law prohibiting the use of birth control was unconstitutional because it violated the "right to marital privacy."

The *Griswold* ruling referred to forms of birth control, like condoms or the pill, that prevent pregnancies from occurring. Another form of birth control is more controversial, for it is utilized after a woman has become pregnant. *Abortion* is a term for ending a pregnancy by removing the fertilized egg (embryo) or developing fetus from a woman's uterus. Until the early 1970s, abortions were nearly always illegal in the United States. There were a few exceptions, such as situations in which giving birth would endanger the woman's life.

During the 1950s and 1960s, if an unmarried girl accidentally became pregnant and did not want the child, or a married woman could not afford

OUR BODIES, OURSELVES

At a women's liberation conference in Boston in 1969, 12 women sat around a table and shared stories about their experiences with "condescending, paternalistic, judgmental and uninformative" doctors. They were amazed at "just how much [they] had to learn about [their] bodies." That day, they decided to research questions about women's health and develop a course for women.

The group, which called itself the Boston Women's Health Book Collective, first produced booklets and workshops for women. In 1971 it published the book *Our Bodies, Ourselves*. The book, which soon became a best-seller, included information about many aspects of women's health and sexuality, including birth control, pregnancy and childbirth, sexual orientation, menopause, and mental health. The book has been revised several times, most recently in October 2011. For more than four decades, this influential book has helped women to understand how their bodies work, and empowered them to participate as informed consumers in their health care decisions.

THE BESTSELLING CLASSIC,
INFORMING AND INSPIRING WOMEN ACROSS GENERATIONS

OUR BODIES, OURSELVES

"Within these pages, you will find the voice of a women's health movement that is based
on shared experience. Listen to it—and add your own."—GLORIA STEINEM

Completely
REVISED
AND
UPDATED

another child, it was not uncommon for that woman to seek an abortion illegally. Those who could afford it traveled out of the country to a place like Sweden, where doctors could perform the abortion procedure safely in a hospital or clinic. Other women attempted to perform the procedure themselves, or took a chance on a local doctor willing to perform the illegal procedure. These back-room abortions were humiliating, often ended in infection, and could be fatal. According to government statistics, during the 1950s and 1960s about a million illegal abortions a year were performed in the United States, and over a thousand women died each year as a result.

Abortion became a divisive issue for all Americans, including those in the women's liberation movement. Some feminists believed that women should have full control over their own bodies, and should therefore have the right to end a pregnancy if they choose. Others believed that the destruction of an embryo or developing fetus was equal to murder, and that it should not be permitted.

In 1972, two young attorneys, Sarah Weddington and Linda Coffee, challenged the abortion law governing the state of Texas. They based their case on the Fourteenth Amendment, arguing that it guaranteed a woman's right to privacy. They maintained that whether a woman carried a pregnancy through to delivery or terminated the pregnancy was her own, private decision. The case, known as *Roe v. Wade*, eventually reached the U.S. Supreme Court.

On January 22, 1973, the Supreme Court, by a vote of seven to two, issued its ruling in *Roe v. Wade*, finding that all state laws barring or restricting abortions during the first three months of pregnancy violated a woman's fundamental right to privacy. Writing for the majority, Justice Harry Blackmun said the right to privacy—which had been established in the *Griswold* case—"is broad enough to encompass a woman's decision whether or not to terminate her pregnancy."

According to the Alan Guttmacher Institute, a New York–based foundation that studies reproductive health issues and advocates for abortion rights, in 1973, after the *Roe v. Wade* decision, there were some 744,000

Pro-choice women demonstrate against Supreme Court nominee Samuel Alito, whom some feared would vote to overturn the *Roe v. Wade* decision that legalized abortion.

abortions performed in the United States. By 1975 the number of abortions performed in the United States exceeded 1 million.

Americans remain deeply divided by the issue of abortion. Vocal (some would say extremist) minorities have staked out uncompromising positions as "pro-choice" (supporting unfettered abortion rights for women) or "pro-life" (opposed to abortion under any circumstance). These groups maintain a steady stream of shrill rhetoric while frequently demonizing those who support the other side. Meanwhile, opinion polls conducted since the 1970s show that most Americans continue to fall somewhere in the middle on the abortion issue, accepting a women's right to have an abortion, but also recognizing certain limitations on that right.

THE EQUAL RIGHTS AMENDMENT

In the early 1970s, many feminists were thrilled at the passage through Congress of the Equal Rights Amendment (ERA) to the U.S. Constitution. This amendment was intended to eliminate all discrimination on the basis of gender; it states in part, "Equality of rights under the law shall not be denied or abridged by the United States or by any State on account of sex."

The U.S. Constitution is the basis of all laws in the United States. It created the framework of government and outlines the relationship of the federal government with the states, citizens, and all people within the country. To change, or amend, the Constitution, a majority of both houses of Congress must vote in favor of the proposed amendment. Then the amendment must be officially approved, or ratified, by the legislatures of three-quarters of the states.

The Equal Rights Amendment had been written by a small group of authors, led by Alice Paul, in 1923. It had been introduced in every Congressional session after that, but was either voted down or never voted upon. In October 1971, Representative Martha Griffiths of Michigan helped get the amendment passed by the House of Representatives. In March 1972, the Senate also passed the amendment. All that was left was for the ERA to be ratified by the 38 of the 50 state legislatures, and it would become a federal law.

At first, the ratifications came quickly. Thirty states had ratified the amendment by the end of 1973. It seemed like the amendment would become law long before a seven-year deadline expired in March 1979. But the pace of ratification suddenly dropped off. Three states ratified during 1974, one in 1975, none in 1976, and one in 1977.

Part of the reason for this was the work of people who opposed the Equal Rights Amendment. One of the most notable of these was a conservative woman named Phyllis Schlafly. To Schlafly, women's rights meant forcing women to give up their traditional roles. Feminists, she believed, "hate men, marriage and children. They are out to destroy morality and the family. They look upon husbands as exploiters, children as an evil to be avoided (by abortion if necessary), and the family as an institution which keeps women in 'second-class citizenship' or even slavery."

Betty Friedan leads a group of women marching in support of the Equal Rights Amendment, 1971.

Activist Phyllis Schafly wearing a "STOP ERA" badge, demonstrates with other women against the Equal Rights Amendment in front of the White House, 1978. Schlafly was no typical stay-at-home mom. She was wealthy, college-educated, and at age 51, after raising her children, she became a lawyer.

In 1973 Schlafly founded a group called STOP ERA to oppose passage of the amendment in states that had not yet ratified. She argued that the ERA would invalidate state laws that require a husband to support his wife and family, making women equally liable for financial responsibilities. Schlafly also contended that the ERA would wipe out state labor laws that benefit women; and that it would eliminate the right of a wife or widow to receive Social Security benefits based on her husband's earnings. Feminists challenged these claims, yet Schlafly's campaign proved to be effective.

With progress on ratification stalled, Congress in 1978 passed a controversial extension of the deadline, bringing it to June 30, 1982. Despite the additional 39 months, no more states ratified the amendment. The extended deadline came and went with the Equal Rights Amendment three states short of becoming federal law. It was a bitter defeat for feminists.

TITLE IX

A more successful law was Title IX, a 1972 amendment of the Civil Rights Act of 1964. Title IX was drafted and introduced by Congresswoman Patsy Mink, with the assistance of Congresswoman Edith Green. The legislation prohibited discrimination on the basis of gender at any school receiving

Title IX provided greater opportunities for women athletes by requiring colleges and high schools to provide athletic programs for females that were equal to those available to males students.

federal funds. It prompted many single-sex schools to become coeducational, and it opened fully all professional studies to women. Limits on women's enrollment in medical schools and law schools were eliminated.

Title IX opened doors for women in colleges and graduate programs. The number of women receiving higher education increased dramatically. In 1970 only 8.4 percent of medical school graduates were women. By 1980, the number had risen to 23 percent. In 1970 only 5.4 percent of law school graduates were women. By 1980, 28.5 percent were women.

Perhaps the effect of Title IX that is most widely known is that it provided greater opportunities in scholastic athletics to women. Coed schools had to sponsor both men's and women's teams. As a result, female athletes gained more opportunities to play for their high school or college.

Other federal legislation passed in the 1970s would provide greater rights and protection to women in the American workforce. In 1972, the Equal Employment Opportunity Act gave the EEOC the authority to file lawsuits against employers that discriminated against women. This law helped stop workplace discrimination.

Another law, the Equal Credit Opportunity Act of 1974, prohibited discrimination based on sex or marital status. This meant a married woman could walk into a bank and open an account in her name. She could sign up for a credit card in her own name. Or she could take out a loan. Before then, banks were allowed to require a husband's signature before they would extend credit, or a woman's credit card could be canceled if she got divorced.

REAPING THE FRUITS OF THEIR LABOR

B y the 1980s, the women's liberation movement had accomplished many important changes that improved the lives of American women. During the late 1960s and early 1970s, feminists had marched with banners saying, "Women of the World, Unite." But by the early 1980s the women's liberation movement had splintered into a variety of women's groups, which each pursued their own goals and agendas.

Nonetheless, despite the lack of unity and leadership, the 1980s witnessed many accomplishments by women. America began to see women achieve positions of responsibility, reaping the benefits of their activism during the 1960s and early 1970s. From 1960 to 1990, attitudes toward women had changed dramatically—at school, at home, and in the workplace.

WOMEN IN UNHEARD OF PLACES

The 1980s saw a dramatic increase in the number of women holding positions of responsibility in government, business, and industry. The rapid increase in numbers was partly due to affirmative action programs, but it was also because women, once given an opportunity, performed as well as men. These working women forever dispelled the myth that women's brains were inferior and that they couldn't cope with stress. Although full equality had not been reached by 1990, significant gains were made.

Sandra Day O'Connor (right) is sworn in as a justice on the U.S. Supreme Court by Chief Justice Warren Burger, while her husband John watches.

There were important "firsts" during the decade. In 1981 Sandra Day O'Connor—who had once been offered a secretarial job in a law firm after graduating first in her Stanford University law school class—was appointed by President Reagan to become the first woman justice on the U.S. Supreme Court. In 1983 physicist Sally Ride became the first woman to fly into space. Other women astronauts soon followed. In 1984 Geraldine Ferraro, an attorney and congresswoman from New York, became the first female candidate on a major political party ticket when she was the vice-presidential nominee of the Democratic Party.

Maya Lin, a 21-year-old architecture student, entered a contest to design the Vietnam War Memorial as part of a class project at Yale University. Her design, which included a granite wall etched with the name of each soldier who died in Vietnam, won the competition. Today, the Vietnam War Memorial is the most visited memorial in Washington, D.C. The facts that Lin, a woman, was a student in a primarily male program, and that her design was chosen reflected the gains women had made.

THINGS KEEP GETTING BETTER

In education, Title IX meant that more women like Maya Lin entered professional studies and were therefore able to take more professional jobs than they had before—not just as architects, lawyers, and doctors, but also as engineers, physicists, and accountants. There were other important changes as well. Sexist language was removed from textbooks. Women's studies programs—what many called "herstory"—were included in college course offerings.

In the workplace, once the new laws were enacted, employers began to view women in a different light. Women in responsible positions began seek greater flexibility from their employers so they wouldn't have to be superwomen in order to both work and have a family, or be forced to leave their job while their children were small. The increase in the number of child care centers, even some in the workplace, simplified the lives of working women. Efforts to equalize pay for women and men who were doing the same jobs helped to lift many women and their families out of poverty and provided better lives for their children.

Attitudes toward sexual harassment in the workplace also changed. In 1980 the EEOC stated that sexual harassment was prohibited by Title VII of the Civil Rights Act. Sexual harassment could include such behaviors as making mean-spirited jokes that made women feel uncomfortable in the office, or a boss making open sexual advances toward someone who worked for him and might be afraid she would lose her job if she did not go along. Thanks to corporate programs educating male and female workers about sexual harassment, by the end of the decade most Americans recognized that sexual

As more women took jobs as television news anchors and journalists, coverage of women's issues increased. Oprah Winfrey—who in the early 1980s had been told by her boss that she was not attractive enough for television work—went on to host an incredibly popular daytime talk show that concentrated on issues relevant to women, such as health, child abuse, alcoholism, and discrimination.

harassment was wrong. The EEOC stood behind women to insure it was kept out of the workplace.

During the 1980s, the way women were portrayed in advertisements and television programming had also changed. Advertisements stopped using women as sex objects or only as wives, mothers, and housekeepers. Female consumers were addressed as if they had intelligence.

In 1991, the U.S. Department of Labor established the Glass Ceiling Commission. This 21-member board studied the barriers that blocked qualified women and minorities from advancing in the corporate workplace. The Commission issued a final report in November 1995. One of the report's recommendations was for corporations to implement programs that would train women and minority employees for senior positions. The report also said that corporations should initiate family-friendly policies and use affirmative action as a tool to ensure that all qualified individuals have equal access and opportunity to compete based on ability and merit. Despite this, according to U.S. Census Bureau statistics from September 2011, women workers earn 77 cents for every dollar earned by men.

FAST FACT

In the 1992 election, the number of women in the U.S. Senate increased from two to six. As a result, 1992 was sometimes called the "Year of the Woman."

In TV shows, women were no longer portrayed as perfect housewives and mothers. Instead, popular shows like *The Mary Tyler Moore Show*, *The Cosby Show*, and *Family Ties* featured female characters who could think, solve problems, and balance careers and families.

CHANGES IN ATTITUDES

Perhaps the most important change in the thirty years between 1960 and 1990 was in the attitude of many men toward the women around them. The laws that were passed to ensure equal treatment for women also helped to open the eyes of reasonable men to the level of discrimination that women had endured. With each passing year, women asserted themselves more and men accepted their movement toward gaining equality.

Men benefitted from women's liberation as well. In the workplace, the rules and regulations that had "protected" women, were extended to men. For example, if women workers were allowed to leave their job to deal with a family emergency, that protection was provided to men as well. As pay increased for professions that had traditionally been filled by women, such as teaching and nursing, more men sought work in those fields. Marriages became partnerships, and men participated more fully in raising and caring for children.

Thanks to the "second wave" of women's rights activists, who took up the fight started by the original suffragists, as the 1990s began American women had greater opportunities than ever before in history. And the changes would continue into the new decade and beyond.

CHAPTER NOTES

p. 9: "the first century of struggle . . ." Ruth Rosen, *The World Split Open: How the Modern Women's Movement Changed America* (New York: Viking, 2000), p. 5.

p. 11: "all men and women are . . ." Declaration of Sentiments, First Women's Rights Convention, Seneca Falls, N.Y. (1848). http://www.usconstitution.net/sentiments.html

p. 12: "It is a downright . . ." Susan B. Anthony, "Speech after Being Convicted of Voting in the 1872 Presidential Election," in Lynne E. Ford, *Encyclopedia of Women and American Politics* (New York: Facts on File, 2008), p. 541.

p. 15: "mystique of feminine fulfillment," Betty Friedan, *The Feminine Mystique* (New York: W. W. Norton, 1963), p. 61.

p. 16: "The suburban housewife . . ." Ibid.

p. 19: "prepare them to be splendid..." W. K. Jordan, quoted in Gail Collins, *When Everything Changed: The Amazing Journey of American Women from 1960 to the Present* (New York: Little, Brown, and Company, 2009), p. 57.

p. 19: "the policy of the Women's Bureau . . ." *To Benefit Women at Work* (Washington, D.C.: U.S. Department of Labor, 1964).

p. 20: "96 percent of married women . . ." Collins, *When Everything Changed*, p. 36.

p. 20: "we can no longer ignore . . ." Friedan, *The Feminine Mystique*, p. 78.

p. 21: "whether one finds it richly rewarding . . ." quoted in Collins, *When Everything Changed*, p. 55.

p. 22: "I came to realize . . ." Friedan, *The Feminine Mystique*, p. 9.

p. 23: "by the time I was . . ." Anna Quindlen, quoted in Rosen, *The World Split Open*, p. 37.

p. 24: "The average white person . . ." Mary King and Casey Hayden, "Women in the Movement" (1965), quoted in Sara Evans, *Personal Politics: The Roots of Women's Liberation in the Civil Rights Movement and the New Left* (New York: Vintage Books, 1980), p. 244.

p. 24: "had all this empathy . . ." quoted in Rosen, *The World Split Open*, p. 131.

p. 26: "a single woman could . . ." Collins, *When Everything Changed*, p. 36.

p. 27: "insist on speaking and acting . . ." Sidney Shallett, quoted in Rosen, *The World Split Open*, p. 65.

p. 30: "[When the law] gives men . . ." Mary O. Eastwood and Pauli Murray, "Jane Crow and the Law: Sex Discrimination and Title VII," *George Washington Law Review* 34 (1965), p. 239.

p. 30: "we are gradually coming to recognize . . ." Eastwood and Murray, "Jane Crow and the Law," p. 256.

p. 31: "I made up my mind . . ." Martha Griffiths, quoted in Collins, *When Everything Changed*, p. 77.

p. 31: "leading advocate of women's rights . . ." Collins, *When Everything Changed*, p. 66.

p. 33: "we had an agency with . . ." Sonia Pressman, quoted in Sheila Tobias, *Faces of Feminism* (Boulder, Colo.: Westview Press, 1997), p. 82.

p. 33: "I would remind them that . . ." Martha Griffiths, quoted in Rosen, *The World Split Open*, p. 73.

p. 34: "underground network of women . . ." Betty Friedan, quoted in Collins, *When Everything Changed*, p. 84.

p. 35: "To take action to bring . . ." National Organization for Women, "Statement of Purpose" (1966). http://www.now.org/history/purpos66.html

p. 36: "My friends and I thought . . ." Meredith Tax, quoted in Rosen, *The World Split Open*, p. 84.

p. 37: "a lifetime of journalists' jokes . . ." Gloria Steinem, *Outrageous Acts and Everyday Rebellions* (New York: Henry Holt, 1983), p. 22–23.

p. 37: "how-to magazine for . . ." Catherine Gourley, *Ms. and the Material Girls* (Minneapolis: Twenty-First Century Books, 2008), p. 23.

p. 39: "that in any society . . ." statement from the Third World Women's Alliance (1968), reprinted in Rosalyn Baxandall and Linda Gordon, *Dear Sisters: Dispatches from the Women's Liberation Movement* (New York: Basic Books, 2000), p. 65.

p. 39: "until you can deal with your own racism . . ." Ibid.

p. 39: "teachers, doctors, nurses, electronic experts . . ." Frances M. Beal, "Double Jeopardy: To Be Black and Female" (1969). http://www.hartford-hwp.com/archives/45a/196.html

p. 41: "We put sex discrimination . . ." Bella Abzug, quoted in Collins, *When Everything Changed*, p. 207.

p. 42: "It would show enormous contempt..." Betty Friedan, *It Changed My Life: Writings on the Women's Movement* (New York: Random House, 1976), p. 171.

p. 42: "right to marital privacy" *Griswold v. Connecticut* (U.S. Supreme Court 381 U.S. 479 (1965), concurring opinion by Justice Arthur Goldberg.

p. 43: "condescending, paternalistic, judgmental and uninformative," Judy Norsigian, et al. "The Boston Women's Health Book Collective and *Our Bodies, Ourselves*: A Brief History and Reflection," *Journal of the American Medical Women's Association* (Winter 1999). http://www.ourbodiesourselves.org/about/jamwa.asp

p. 43: "just how much we had . . ." Ibid.

p. 44: "is broad enough to encompass . . ." *Roe v. Wade* (U.S. Supreme Court 410 U.S. 113 (1973), majority opinion by Justice Harry Blackmun.

p. 44: Statistics on 1973 and 1975 abortion totals credited to the Alan Guttmacher Institute reprinted in Willard Cates, et. al, "The Public Health Impact of Legal Abortion: 30 Years Later," *Perspectives on Sexual and Reproductive Health* 35, no. 1 (January/February 2003).

p. 45: "Equality of rights under . . ." Ruth Bader Ginsburg, "The Need for the Equal Rights Amendment," *ABA Journal* (September 1973), p. 1018.

p. 46: "hate men, marriage and children." Phyllis Schlafly, quoted in Rosen, *The World Split Open*, p. 39.

CHRONOLOGY

1848: The first Women's Rights Convention is held in Seneca Falls, New York on July 19-20. Under the leadership of Elizabeth Cady Stanton and Lucretia Mott, a Declaration of Sentiments is passed. It includes the revolutionary idea that women deserved the vote.

1920: On August 26, 1920, the Nineteenth Amendment, granting women the right to vote, is added to the Constitution of the United States.

1961: President John F. Kennedy forms the President's Commission on the Status of Women (PCSW). Two years later, the commission issues a report that recommends ending discriminatory practices against women.

1963: Betty Friedan's book, *The Feminine Mystique*, is published on February 25. The book is credited with re-starting the women's rights movement; on June 10, President Kennedy signs the Equal Pay Act into law. The new legislation mandates that women and men should be paid the same for doing similar jobs.

1964: The 1964 Civil Rights Act is enacted on July 2 prohibiting discrimination on the workplace on the basis of race, color, religion, sex, or national origin. This act is the most sweeping women's rights legislation to date. It creates the Equal Employment Opportunity Commission.

1966: The National Organization for Women (NOW) grows out of a meeting of the Commission on the Status of Women. The organization has its founding conference on October 29-30. Betty Friedan is chosen as its first president.

1968: The first National Women's Liberation Conference is held in Washington, D.C., in January, on the same day as a protest against the Vietnam War led by former congresswoman Jeannette Rankin. The women's liberation conference spawns activities by radical feminists that become known as the women's liberation movement.

1970: Publication of *Our Bodies, Ourselves*, a book developed by the Boston Women's Health Book Cooperative to inform women about their health; on August 26, the Women's Strike for Equality celebrates the fiftieth anniversary of the passing of the Nineteenth Amendment.

Some 20,000 women march in New York City, with thousands more marching in other cities.

1971: The National Women's Political Caucus is formed at a conference on July 10-11. Its purpose is to support women candidates for election to local and national offices.

1972: The first issue of *Ms. Magazine* is published in January; in March 1972 the Equal Rights Amendment is passed by both houses of Congress and is sent to the states for ratification; Title IX of the Education Amendments is enacted on June 23. This legislation prohibits gender discrimination in any school that receives federal funds; Phyllis Schlafly founds STOP ERA, a conservative organization dedicated to preventing ratification of the Equal Rights Amendment.

1973: On January 22, the *Roe v. Wade* Supreme Court Decision gives women the right to choose abortion during the first trimester of a pregnancy.

1976: Representative Henry Hyde succeeds in passing an amendment disallowing use of Medicaid money for abortions. This eliminates abortion as an option for many poor women.

1978: For the first time there are more women entering college than men.

1980: The Equal Employment Opportunity Commission decrees that sexual harassment is prohibited by Title VII of the 1964 Civil Rights Act.

1981: On July 7 Sandra Day O'Connor becomes the first woman to serve as a justice on the U.S. Supreme Court.

1982: The June 30 deadline for the Equal Rights Amendment to become part of the U.S. Constitution passes without enough states voting to ratify the amendment.

1983: NASA astronaut Sally Ride becomes the first American woman in space.

1984: Geraldine Ferraro becomes the first woman to run as the vice presidential candidate for a major party.

1985: The *New York Times* agrees to use the title "Ms." instead of "Mrs."

GLOSSARY

advocate—a person who speaks out for a cause or another person.

amendment—a legal change to the U.S. Constitution.

baby boom—term used to describe the increase in the number of babies born in the years after World War II. The "baby boom generation" typically refers to children born in the United States between 1946 and 1964.

civil rights—the rights of a citizen to political and social freedom and equality.

coeducational—education that open to both males and females.

discrimination—the unjust or prejudicial treatment of people based on sex, race, religion, age, or another category.

federal—relating to the central government of the United States.

feminism—the advocacy of achieving social, political, and economic equality between the sexes.

paternalism—to act for the good of another person without that person's consent, as a father would for his children. (The English word *paternalism* comes from the Latin *pater*, meaning to act like a father.) Paternalistic behavior often includes restricting the subordinates' freedom or responsibilities "for their own good."

ratification—the act of giving formal consent to a measure; the act of making it officially valid.

suffrage—the right to vote.

FURTHER READING

FOR YOUNGER READERS

Bohannon, Lisa Fredericksen. *Woman's Work: The Story of Betty Freidan.* Greensboro, N.C.: Morgan Reynolds Publishing, 2004.

Gourley, Catherine. *Ms. And the Material Girls.* Minneapolis: Twenty-First Century Books, 2008.

Marcello, Patricia Cronin. *Gloria Steinem, a Biography.* Westport, Conn.: Greenwood Press, 2004.

Schomp, Virginia. *The Women's Movement.* New York: Marshall Cavendish Benchmark, 2007.

Wright, Susan. *The Civil Rights Act of 1964: Landmark Antidiscrimination Legislation.* New York: Rosen Publishing Group, 2006.

FOR OLDER READERS

Collins, Gail. *When Everything Changed: The Amazing Journey of American Women from 1960 to the Present.* New York: Little, Brown, and Co., 2009.

Critchlow, Donald T. *Phyllis Schlafly and Grassroots Conservatism: A Woman's Crusade.* Princeton, N.J.: Princeton University Press, 2005.

Stansell, Christine. *The Feminist Promise: 1792 to the Present.* New York: Modern Library, 2010.

Strebeigh, Fred. *Equal: Women Reshape American Law.* New York: W.W. Norton, 2009.

Walton, Mary. *A Woman's Crusade: Alice Paul and the Battle for the Ballot.* New York: Palgrave Macmillan, 2010.

INTERNET RESOURCES

http://scriptorium.lib.duke.edu/wlm/blkmanif/#

Text of a landmark essay by the radical African-American feminist Frances M. Beal, "Double Jeopardy: To be Black and Female."

http://www.now.org/history/purpos66.html

The National Organization for Women's 1966 "Statement of Purpose" is available on NOW's official website.

http://www.ourbodiesourselves.org/about/history.asp

This history of the Boston Women's Health Book Collective is available on the organization's website.

http://memory.loc.gov/ammem/awhhtml/aw03e/aw03e.html

This site features a Library of Congress essay on American women. Text and photos make up "The Long Road to Equality: What Women Won from the ERA Ratification Effort."

http://www.equalrightsamendment.org

This website features background information on the ERA. It also includes the ERA's current status in the U.S. Congress and in unratified states.

INDEX

Numbers in **bold italics** refer to captions.

CONTRIBUTORS

TERRY CATASÚS JENNINGS is now a freelance writer. Her work has been published in *The Washington Post*, *Long Island Newsday*, *The Reston Connection*, and *Ranger Rick*. She is a contributor to the National Science Resource Center's SCIENCE AND TECHNOLOGY FOR CHILDREN series. Before her freelance career, however, Terry was in the first group of women hired by AT&T into their engineering department. She experienced the pay discrimination she details in this book and was part of a settlement between the EEOC and AT&T. When her children were born, she chose to stay home because of lack of good child care. It was at this time when, in addition to significant volunteer work, she began her freelancing career. She lives in Reston, Virginia.

Senior Consulting Editor **A. PAGE HARRINGTON** is executive director of the Sewall-Belmont House and Museum, on Capitol Hill in Washington, D.C. The Sewall-Belmont House celebrates women's progress toward equality—and explores the evolving role of women and their contributions to society—through educational programs, tours, exhibits, research, and publications.

The historic National Woman's Party (NWP), a leader in the campaign for equal rights and women's suffrage, owns, maintains, and interprets the Sewall-Belmont House and Museum. One of the premier women's history sites in the country, this National Historic Landmark houses an extensive collection of suffrage banners, archives, and artifacts documenting the continuing effort by women and men of all races, religions, and backgrounds to win voting rights and equality for women under the law.

The Sewall-Belmont House and Museum and the National Woman's Party are committed to preserving the legacy of Alice Paul, founder of the NWP and author of the Equal Rights Amendment, and telling the untold stories for the benefit of scholars, current and future generations of Americans, and all the world's citizens.